First published 1975 by Purnell Books,
Berkshire House, Queen Street, Maidenhead.
Designed and produced for Purnell Books by
Intercontinental Book Productions
Copyright © 1975 Intercontinental Book Productions
Printed in Belgium by H. Proost & Cie
SBN 361 03182 3

MAKE YOUR OWN
MODELS AND TOYS THAT GO

Models and text by Brian Edwards

Illustrated by Ron Brown

Photography by Richard Sharpe Studios

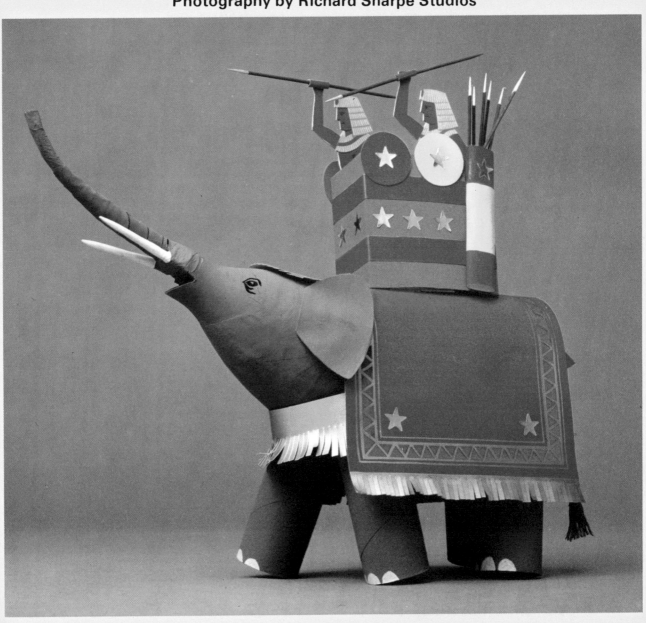

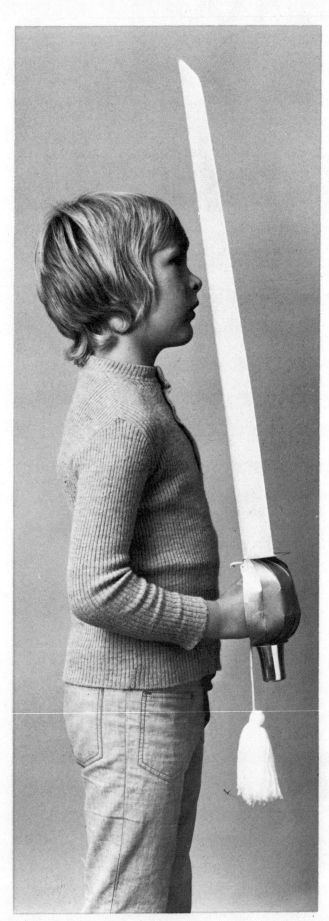

INTRODUCTION

Everyone feels good about creating something from nothing and in *Make Your Own* we show you how. Every project has been designed by experts especially for children to make with little or no help from adults. All items are made from materials which are readily found in the home, such as egg boxes, oddments of paper, grocery boxes and cereal packets.

It is not necessary to follow exactly the colours used in this book to decorate the models. Each child should be encouraged to use colours to suit individual taste and at the same time, learn from the simple principles involved in the book how to create other exciting projects.

Best results will be achieved by using the materials as listed and it should be stressed that care should be taken when using certain tools necessary for some projects in this book.

In all grid patterns throughout this book, 1 square = 2.5 cm.

Contents

Go-Yo and Spinning Top

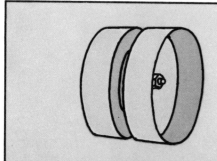

Punch a hole in centre of each lid. Place washer between two lids and push bolt through all three. Screw nut on tightly.

1

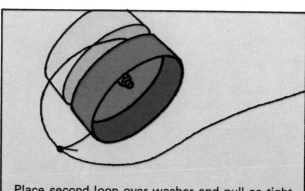

Paint Go-Yo and tie a small loop at end of string. Tie a loop at other end of string with a slip knot.

2

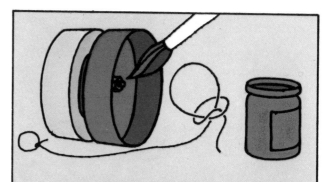

Place second loop over washer and pull as tight as you can.

3

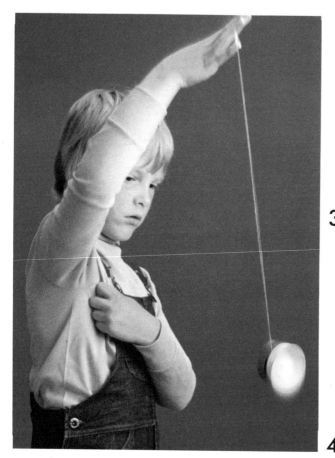

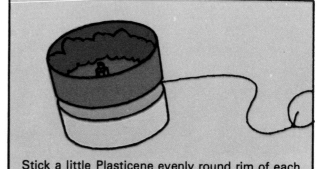

Stick a little Plasticene evenly round rim of each jar lid. Wind string tightly round washer and Go-Yo away!

4

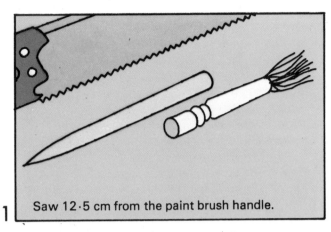

1 Saw 12·5 cm from the paint brush handle.

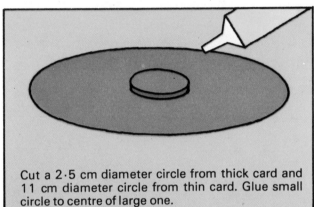

2 Cut a 2·5 cm diameter circle from thick card and 11 cm diameter circle from thin card. Glue small circle to centre of large one.

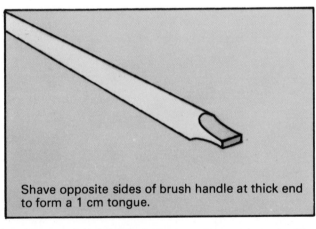

3 Shave opposite sides of brush handle at thick end to form a 1 cm tongue.

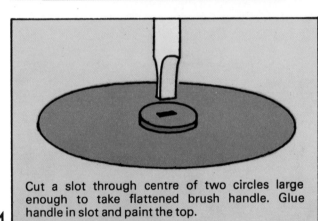

4 Cut a slot through centre of two circles large enough to take flattened brush handle. Glue handle in slot and paint the top.

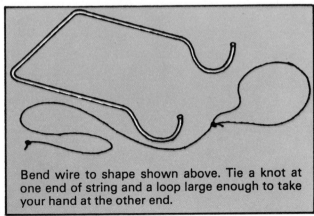

5 Bend wire to shape shown above. Tie a knot at one end of string and a loop large enough to take your hand at the other end.

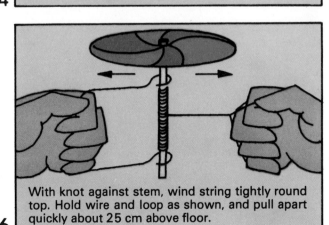

6 With knot against stem, wind string tightly round top. Hold wire and loop as shown, and pull apart quickly about 25 cm above floor.

Play Pingball

YOU WILL NEED:
hardboard: approx. 55 x 45 cm · strong glue
card: approx. 60 x 45 cm · 10 marbles
large toothpaste box
pencil or dowel, 15 cm long
14 tube or small bottle caps
cotton reel · 8 assorted small boxes
3 rubber bands · craft knife · steel rule
2 spent matchsticks · scissors

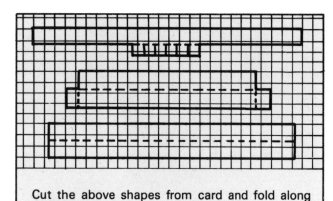

1 Cut the above shapes from card and fold along dotted lines.

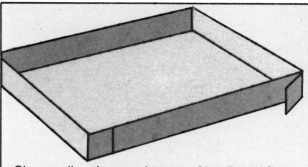

2 Glue smaller pieces to bottom of hardboard (long folds level with edge of board). Bend up and glue flaps on ends to back of sides.

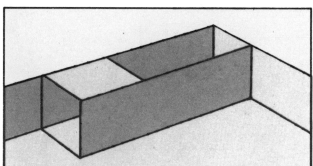

3 Cut one end and three-quarters of top from toothpaste box. Glue to corner of the tray you have made.

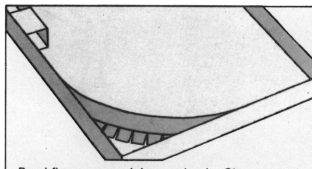

4 Bend flaps on remaining card strip. Glue one end to side wall near box and other to end wall of tray. Glue flaps to base.

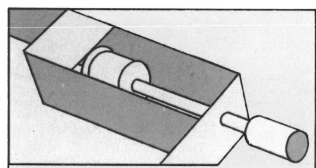

5 Make a hole through end of box and tray. Push pencil through. Glue cotton reel on one end and a bottle cap on other.

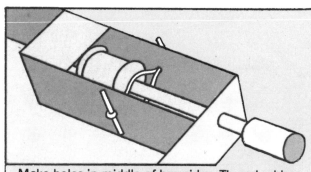

6 Make holes in middle of box sides. Thread rubber band through. Secure ends with matchsticks. Push cotton reel through rubber band.

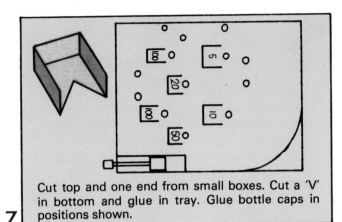

7 Cut top and one end from small boxes. Cut a 'V' in bottom and glue in tray. Glue bottle caps in positions shown.

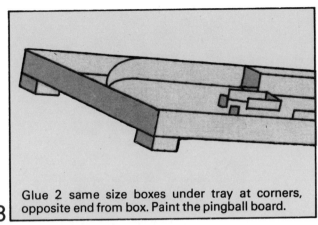

8 Glue 2 same size boxes under tray at corners, opposite end from box. Paint the pingball board.

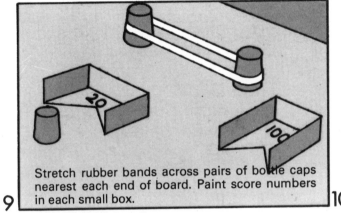

9 Stretch rubber bands across pairs of bottle caps nearest each end of board. Paint score numbers in each small box.

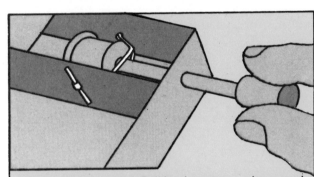

10 Put a marble in box. Pull back cotton reel gun and let go. Marble must hit left wall before you can score. Fire all marbles, count score.

Here we go Round

YOU WILL NEED:
a round tin: approx. 12·5 cm diameter × 2·5 cm deep
round cheese box or tin lid: approx.
 12·5 cm diameter × 1 cm deep
round plastic ice cream or yoghurt cup
cotton reel · drawing pin · ball point pen · Sellotape
rubber band: 5-7·5 cm long · strong glue · pencil · nail
scissors · ruler · hammer · thin card: approx. 20 × 20 cm
bradawl or round file · pencil stub · paints · pliers
sticky cut-out paper shapes
thin wire 15 cm long

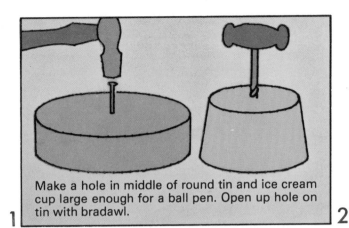

Make a hole in middle of round tin and ice cream cup large enough for a ball pen. Open up hole on tin with bradawl.

1

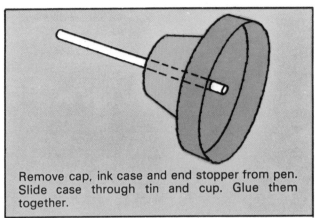

Remove cap, ink case and end stopper from pen. Slide case through tin and cup. Glue them together.

2

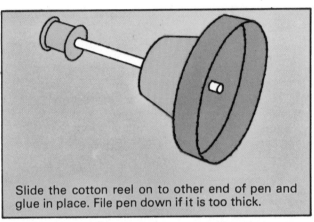

Slide the cotton reel on to other end of pen and glue in place. File pen down if it is too thick.

3

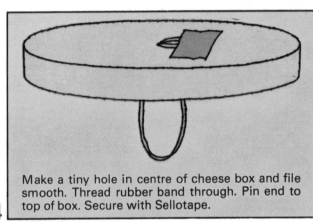

Make a tiny hole in centre of cheese box and file smooth. Thread rubber band through. Pin end to top of box. Secure with Sellotape.

4

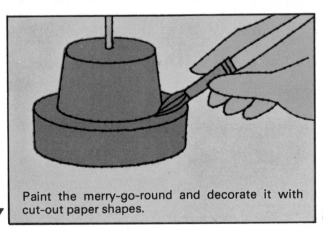

Bend wire into a hook and use it to pull rubber band through the pen case. Loop bottom end round a pencil stub.

5

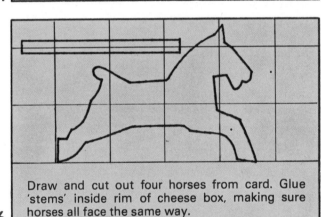

Draw and cut out four horses from card. Glue 'stems' inside rim of cheese box, making sure horses all face the same way.

6

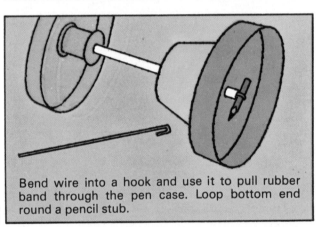

Paint the merry-go-round and decorate it with cut-out paper shapes.

7

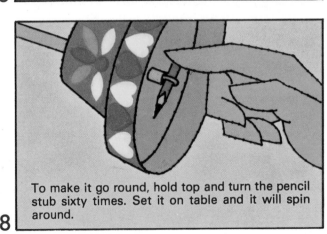

To make it go round, hold top and turn the pencil stub sixty times. Set it on table and it will spin around.

8

Katie the Crawling Caterpillar

YOU WILL NEED:
round tin: approx. 10 cm diameter x 4·5 cm deep
cotton reel · yoghurt cup · scissors
coloured paper: approx. 22 x 55 cm
pliers · pipe cleaner · hammer and nail
2 pieces piano wire, 75 cm and 29 cm long
paints · electrician's tape · protractor

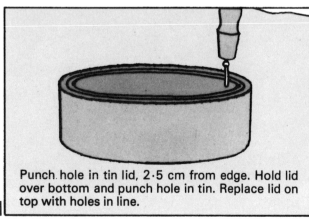

1 Punch hole in tin lid, 2·5 cm from edge. Hold lid over bottom and punch hole in tin. Replace lid on top with holes in line.

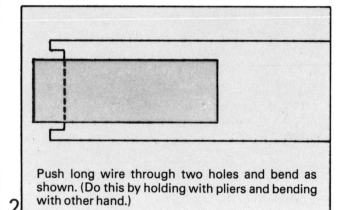

2 Push long wire through two holes and bend as shown. (Do this by holding with pliers and bending with other hand.)

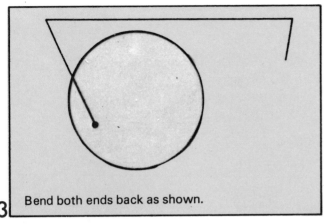

3 Bend both ends back as shown.

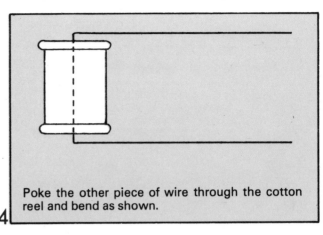

4 Poke the other piece of wire through the cotton reel and bend as shown.

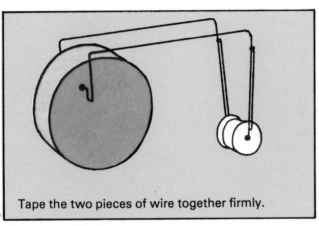

5 Tape the two pieces of wire together firmly.

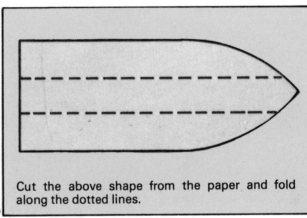

6 Cut the above shape from the paper and fold along the dotted lines.

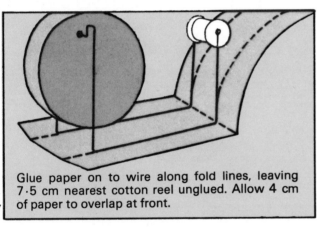

7 Glue paper on to wire along fold lines, leaving 7·5 cm nearest cotton reel unglued. Allow 4 cm of paper to overlap at front.

8 Make 2 holes in yoghurt cup, 1·25 cm from end. Poke pipe cleaners through and bend up ends.

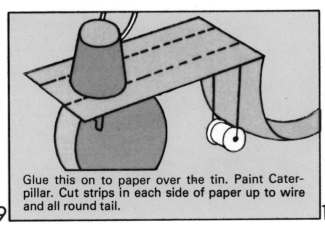

9 Glue this on to paper over the tin. Paint Caterpillar. Cut strips in each side of paper up to wire and all round tail.

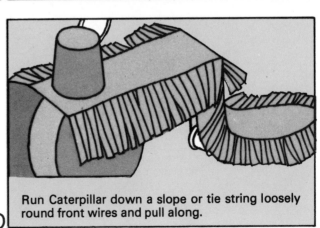

10 Run Caterpillar down a slope or tie string loosely round front wires and pull along.

Stand to Attention

YOU WILL NEED:
cardboard tube: approx. 35 cm long
cardboard box: approx. 5 × 12·5 × 10 cm
thin card · glue · scissors
craft knife · paints

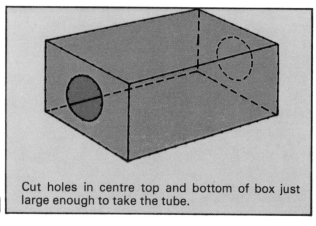

1 Cut holes in centre top and bottom of box just large enough to take the tube.

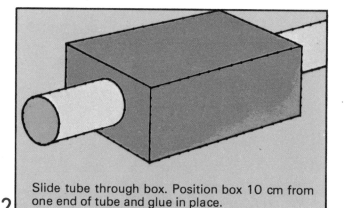

2 Slide tube through box. Position box 10 cm from one end of tube and glue in place.

3 Cut the above shapes from the card.

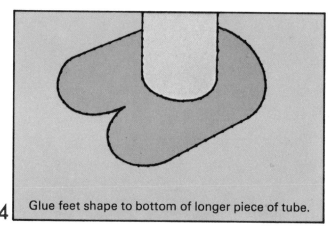

4 Glue feet shape to bottom of longer piece of tube.

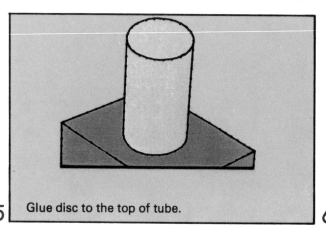

5 Glue disc to the top of tube.

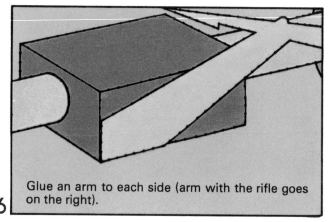

6 Glue an arm to each side (arm with the rifle goes on the right).

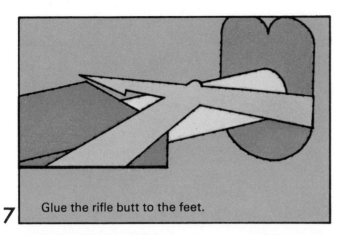

7 Glue the rifle butt to the feet.

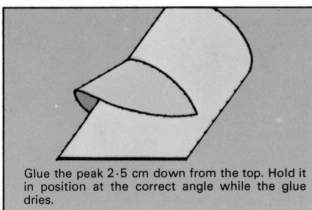

8 Glue the peak 2·5 cm down from the top. Hold it in position at the correct angle while the glue dries.

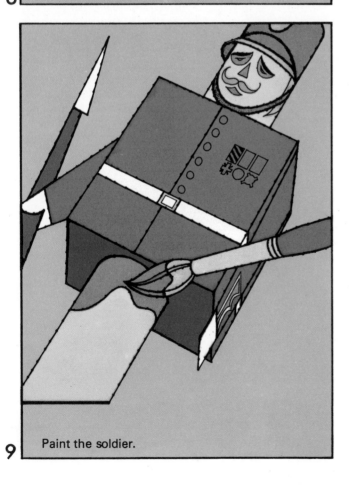

9 Paint the soldier.

Drawbridge

YOU WILL NEED:
2 cardboard boxes: approx. 5 x 17·5 x 25 cm
glue · Sellotape · pliers · pencil
thick card: approx. 10 x 22 cm
stiff wire 25 cm long · thread 60 cm long
steel rule · paints (preferably Emulsion)
craft knife

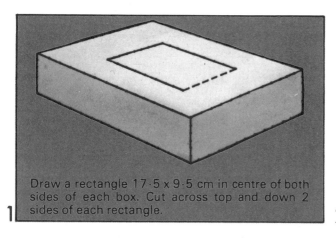

1 Draw a rectangle 17·5 x 9·5 cm in centre of both sides of each box. Cut across top and down 2 sides of each rectangle.

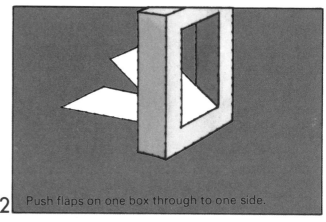

2 Push flaps on one box through to one side.

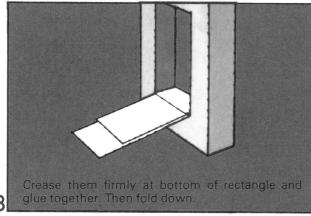

3 Crease them firmly at bottom of rectangle and glue together. Then fold down.

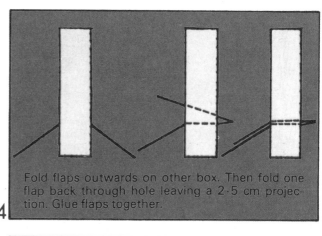

4 Fold flaps outwards on other box. Then fold one flap back through hole leaving a 2·5 cm projection. Glue flaps together.

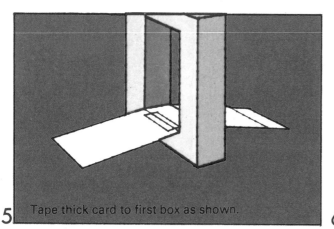

5 Tape thick card to first box as shown.

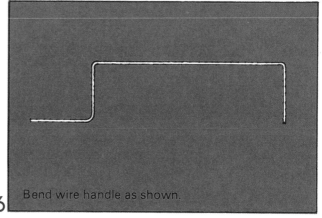

6 Bend wire handle as shown.

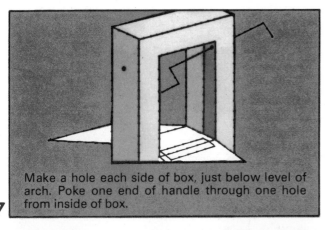

Make a hole each side of box, just below level of arch. Poke one end of handle through one hole from inside of box.

7

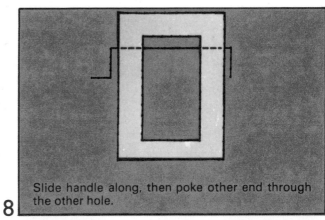

Slide handle along, then poke other end through the other hole.

8

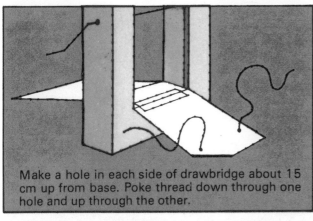

Make a hole in each side of drawbridge about 15 cm up from base. Poke thread down through one hole and up through the other.

9

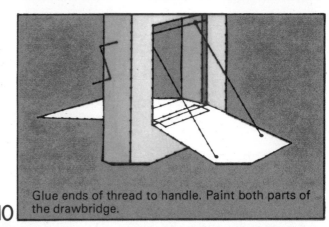

Glue ends of thread to handle. Paint both parts of the drawbridge.

10

The Balancing Clown Act

YOU WILL NEED:
stiff card: approx. 20 cm square
compass · craft knife · cocktail stick
2 large coins the same size · glue
drinking straw · paints · pencil
thread 240 cm long
tracing paper: approx. 20 cm square
carbon paper · Sellotape

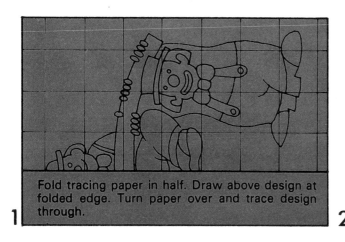

Fold tracing paper in half. Draw above design at folded edge. Turn paper over and trace design through.

1

Unfold paper and tape it to card. Insert carbon paper. Trace down the three clowns with a sharp pencil.

2

3 Cut out shape from card. Slot between middle clown's legs should be 2·5 cm long and 1·25 cm wide.

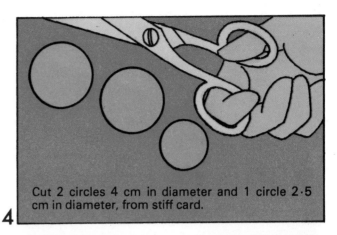

4 Cut 2 circles 4 cm in diameter and 1 circle 2·5 cm in diameter, from stiff card.

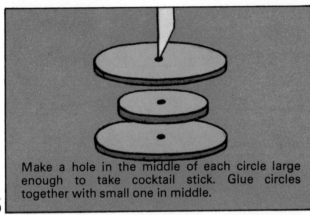

5 Make a hole in the middle of each circle large enough to take cocktail stick. Glue circles together with small one in middle.

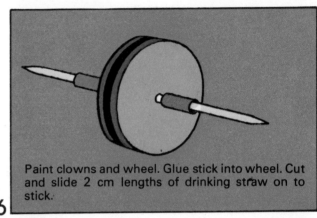

6 Paint clowns and wheel. Glue stick into wheel. Cut and slide 2 cm lengths of drinking straw on to stick.

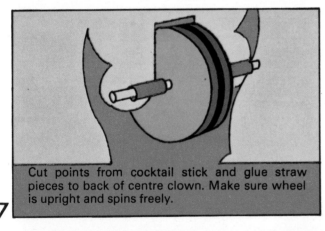

7 Cut points from cocktail stick and glue straw pieces to back of centre clown. Make sure wheel is upright and spins freely.

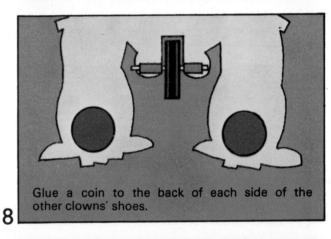

8 Glue a coin to the back of each side of the other clowns' shoes.

9 Tie thread to two chairs so that one end is higher than the other. Send the balancing trio down the high wire.

The White Knight...

YOU WILL NEED:
white paper: approx. 30 x 25 cm
plastic bottle top (slightly tapering at top)
bamboo cane
newspaper · strong glue · scissors
thin card: approx. 7·5 x 10 cm · craft knife
plastic bottle, 6 cm wide
small feather · jar lid
cocktail stick

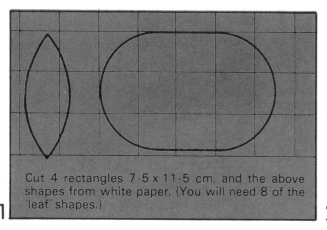

1 Cut 4 rectangles 7·5 x 11·5 cm., and the above shapes from white paper. (You will need 8 of the 'leaf' shapes.)

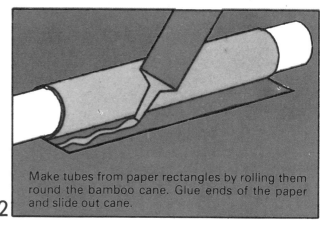

2 Make tubes from paper rectangles by rolling them round the bamboo cane. Glue ends of the paper and slide out cane.

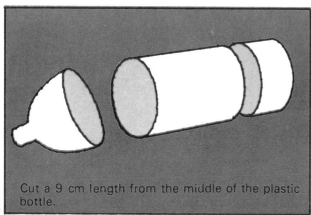

3 Cut a 9 cm length from the middle of the plastic bottle.

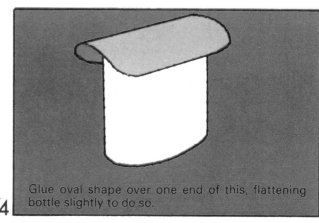

4 Glue oval shape over one end of this, flattening bottle slightly to do so.

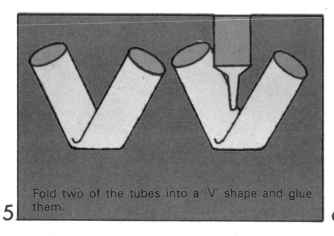

5 Fold two of the tubes into a 'V' shape and glue them.

6 Glue top of straight tubes inside plastic bottle. Glue folded tubes to sides of bottle and stuff bottle with newspaper.

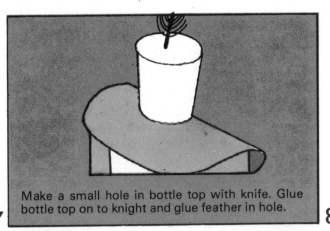

7 Make a small hole in bottle top with knife. Glue bottle top on to knight and glue feather in hole.

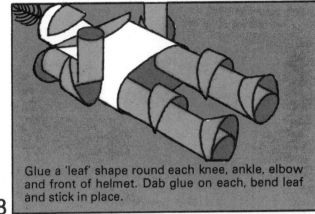

8 Glue a 'leaf' shape round each knee, ankle, elbow and front of helmet. Dab glue on each, bend leaf and stick in place.

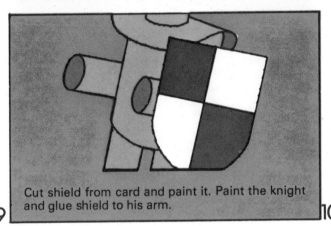

9 Cut shield from card and paint it. Paint the knight and glue shield to his arm.

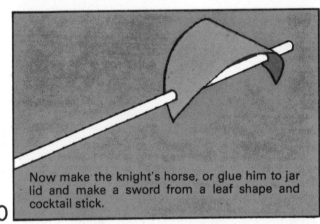

10 Now make the knight's horse, or glue him to jar lid and make a sword from a leaf shape and cocktail stick.

...and his Faithful Charger

YOU WILL NEED:
white paper: approx. 40 x 55 cm
plastic fruit squash bottle
bamboo cane: approx. 72 cm long
4 plastic bottle caps (slightly tapering)
block of wood: approx. 30 x 13 x 1·5 cm
white Emulsion paint · gummed tape
strong glue · newspaper · Sellotape
toilet roll tube · craft knife · paints
scissors · 15 cm coarse string · comb
dowel 60 cm long · fine saw · compass
pencil · ruler

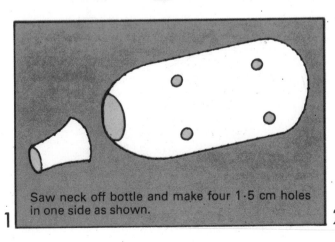

1 Saw neck off bottle and make four 1·5 cm holes in one side as shown.

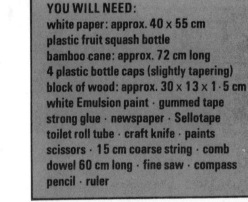

2 Saw cane into four. Make alternate cuts at a 45° angle so that each piece has one angled end.

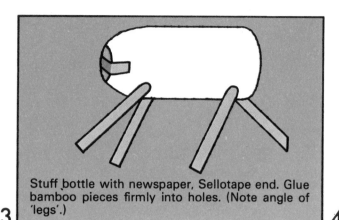

Stuff bottle with newspaper, Sellotape end. Glue bamboo pieces firmly into holes. (Note angle of 'legs'.)

3

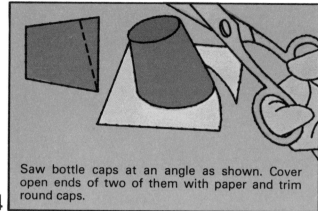

Saw bottle caps at an angle as shown. Cover open ends of two of them with paper and trim round caps.

4

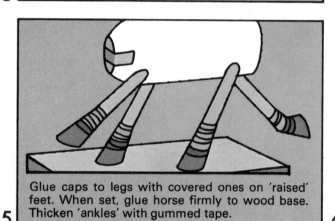

Glue caps to legs with covered ones on 'raised' feet. When set, glue horse firmly to wood base. Thicken 'ankles' with gummed tape.

5

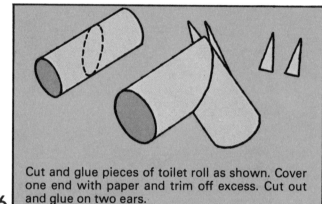

Cut and glue pieces of toilet roll as shown. Cover one end with paper and trim off excess. Cut out and glue on two ears.

6

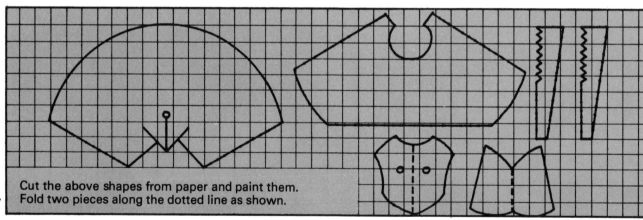

Cut the above shapes from paper and paint them. Fold two pieces along the dotted line as shown.

7

Glue on 'head' and paint horse. Wrap large shape with hole in middle round neck and glue in place.

8

Glue other large piece over horse's rump by overlapping two pointed pieces and gluing. Glue two large flaps over them.

9

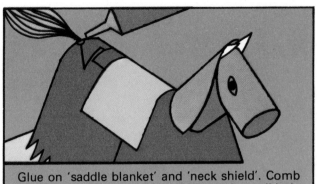

10 Glue on 'saddle blanket' and 'neck shield'. Comb out one end of string and glue through small hole at back for tail.

11 Glue on face shield and cut out eye holes. Flatten thighs of knight and glue on to the saddle.

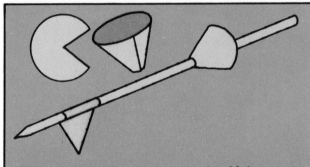

12 Sharpen dowel to a point and paint. Make a cone from 'C' shaped paper. Slide on to dowel and glue in place. Glue on pennant.

13 Glue lance to right arm. Glue reins over left arm and each side of horse's nose. Glue shield to knight's left arm.

Museum Piece

YOU WILL NEED:
cardboard tube: approx. 18 cm long
toilet roll tube · rubber band
thin card: approx. 23 x 12·5 cm
cardboard box: approx. 11·5 x 7·5 x 5 cm
round cheese box or 2 tin lids: approx.
   12·5 cm across
2 spent matches · scissors · Sellotape
paints
small pieces of paper: approx. 5 x 2·5 cm

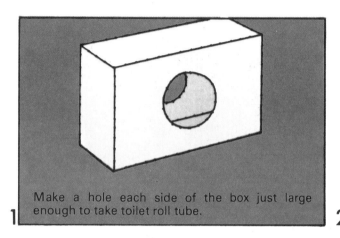

1 Make a hole each side of the box just large enough to take toilet roll tube.

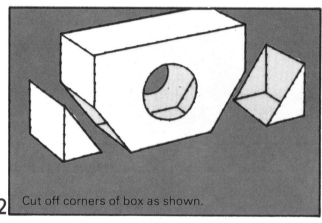

2 Cut off corners of box as shown.

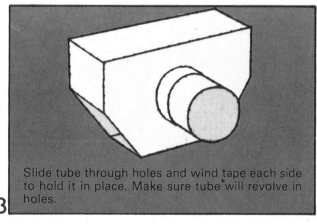

3 Slide tube through holes and wind tape each side to hold it in place. Make sure tube will revolve in holes.

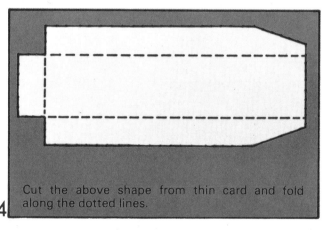

4 Cut the above shape from thin card and fold along the dotted lines.

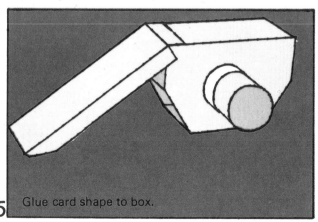

5 Glue card shape to box.

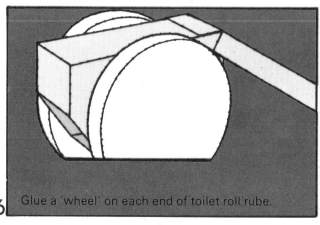

6 Glue a 'wheel' on each end of toilet roll rube.

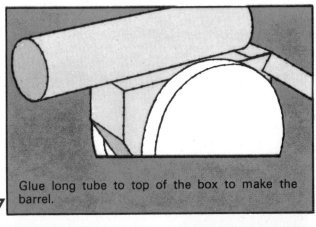

Glue long tube to top of the box to make the barrel.

7

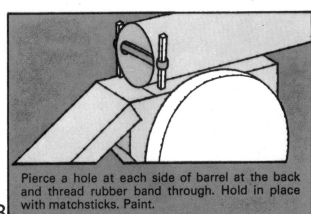

Pierce a hole at each side of barrel at the back and thread rubber band through. Hold in place with matchsticks. Paint.

8

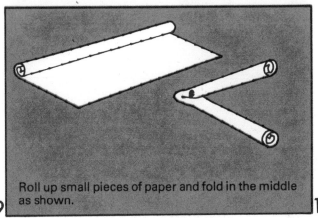

Roll up small pieces of paper and fold in the middle as shown.

9

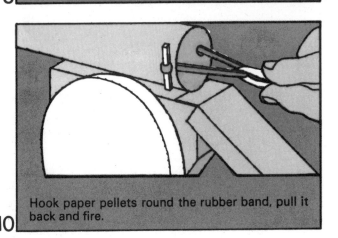

Hook paper pellets round the rubber band, pull it back and fire.

10

Tribal Hunting Elephant

YOU WILL NEED:
1 plastic fruit squash bottle
4 toilet roll tubes · paint brush handles
thin card: approx. 15 x 20 cm
strong glue · craft knife · sandpaper
cardboard box: approx. 9 x 5 x 10 cm
paper: approx. 30 x 30 cm
10 cocktail sticks · paints
thick wire flex 15 cm long
dowel: 0·5 x 15 cm
scissors · Sellotape or electrician's tape
fine saw · thick string 15 cm long

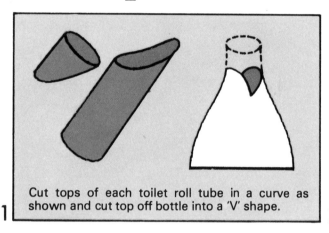

1 Cut tops of each toilet roll tube in a curve as shown and cut top off bottle into a 'V' shape.

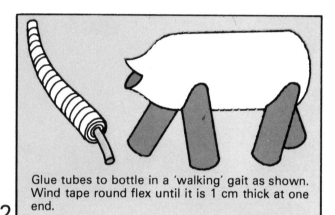

2 Glue tubes to bottle in a 'walking' gait as shown. Wind tape round flex until it is 1 cm thick at one end.

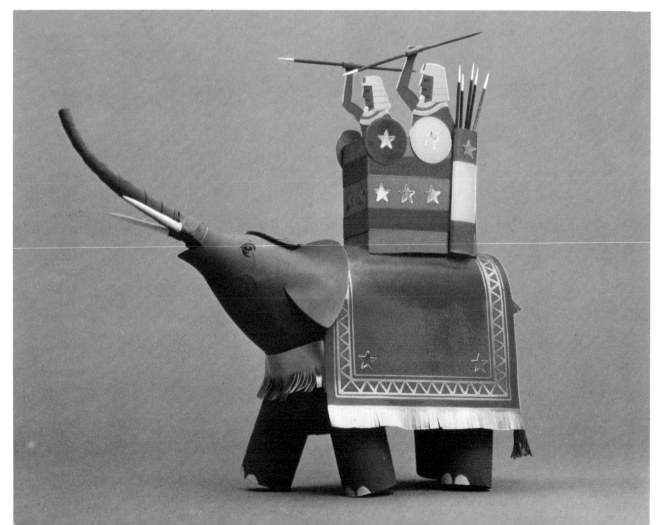

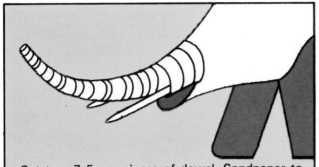

Cut two 7.5 cm pieces of dowel. Sandpaper to a point. Glue flex inside bottle. Glue dowels each side. Wind tape round trunk, tusks and neck.

3

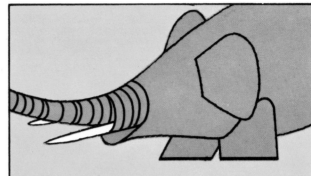

Cut two paper ears as shown and glue in place. Glue string 'tail' to back and paint the elephant.

4

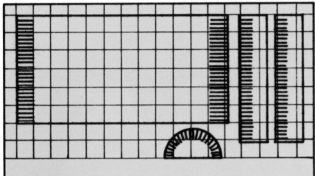

Cut the above shapes from paper and paint them. Cut 1 cm slits along the edges as shown.

5

Glue one strip round neck and another round back of elephant. Glue semicircle on to head and the 'carpet' over elephant's back.

6

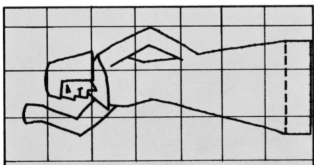

Cut top and bottom from box. Curve one end to fit back. Roll and glue an 8 x 5.5 cm piece of paper. Flatten slightly and glue to side. Paint.

7

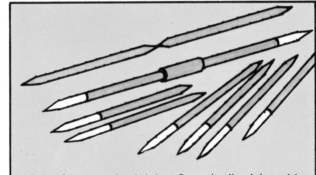

Make 2 spears by joining 2 cocktail sticks with tape, then paint. Paint remaining cocktail sticks.

8

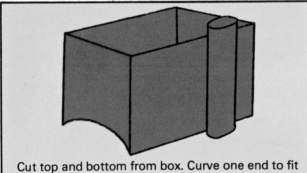

Cut out 2 soldiers with 1 cm tabs on feet, from card. Cut out 4 discs, 3 cm in diameter, to make shields. Paint pieces.

9

Glue box to elephant's back. Bend tabs and glue soldiers inside box. Glue spears and shields in place.

10

29

Ceremonial Sword

YOU WILL NEED:
thick card: approx. 4 x 75 cm
thin card: approx. 15 x 7·5 cm
thick paper: approx. 16·5 x 20 cm
toilet roll tube · craft knife · steel rule
skein of wool · scissors
cord: approx. 30 cm long · sandpaper
large plastic bottle top
scrap card: approx. 12·5 x 7·5 cm
gold and silver paint · pencil · set square

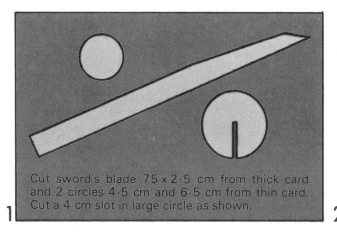

1 Cut sword's blade 75 x 2·5 cm from thick card and 2 circles 4·5 cm and 6·5 cm from thin card. Cut a 4 cm slot in large circle as shown.

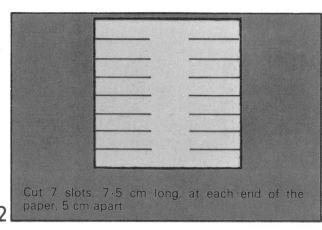

2 Cut 7 slots, 7·5 cm long, at each end of the paper, 5 cm apart.

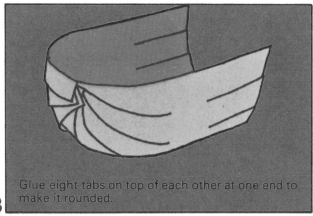

3 Glue eight tabs on top of each other at one end to make it rounded.

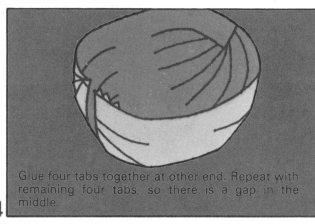

4 Glue four tabs together at other end. Repeat with remaining four tabs, so there is a gap in the middle.

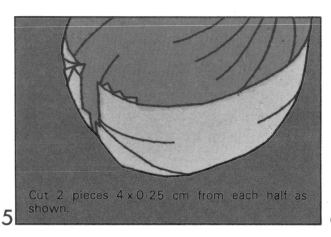

5 Cut 2 pieces 4 x 0·25 cm from each half as shown.

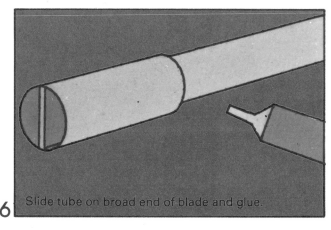

6 Slide tube on broad end of blade and glue.

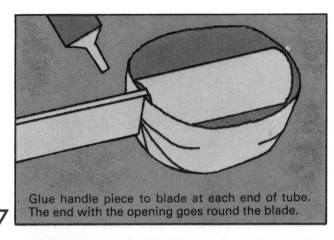

7 Glue handle piece to blade at each end of tube. The end with the opening goes round the blade.

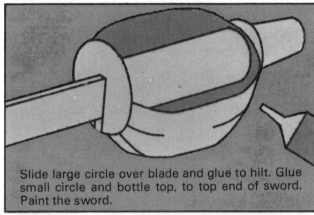

8 Slide large circle over blade and glue to hilt. Glue small circle and bottle top, to top end of sword. Paint the sword.

9 Wind wool round scrap card. Slide cord under wool at one end and tie. Cut wool at other end.

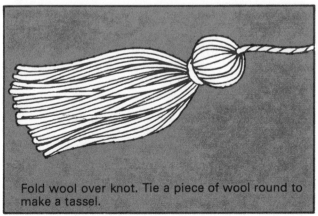

10 Fold wool over knot. Tie a piece of wool round to make a tassel.

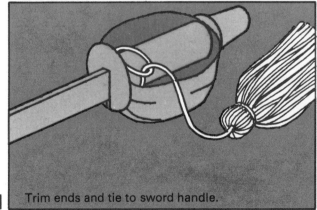

11 Trim ends and tie to sword handle.

Captain's Shako

YOU WILL NEED:
large sheet of stiff white paper
thin card: approx. 20 × 35 cm
glue · compass · scissors · craft knife
steel rule · pins · Sellotape · paints

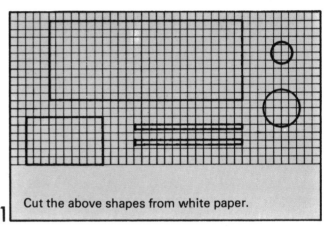

1 Cut the above shapes from white paper.

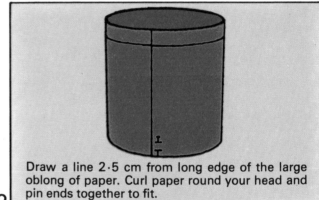

2 Draw a line 2·5 cm from long edge of the large oblong of paper. Curl paper round your head and pin ends together to fit.

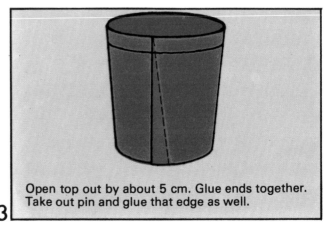

3 Open top out by about 5 cm. Glue ends together. Take out pin and glue that edge as well.

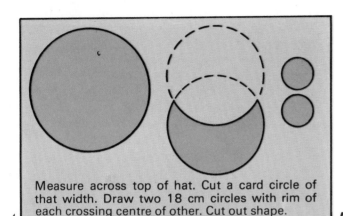

Measure across top of hat. Cut a card circle of that width. Draw two 18 cm circles with rim of each crossing centre of other. Cut out shape.

4

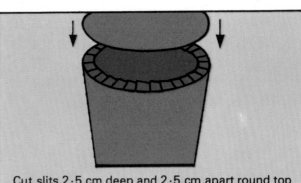

Cut slits 2·5 cm deep and 2·5 cm apart round top of hat. Bend tabs inwards and glue the card circle on to them.

5

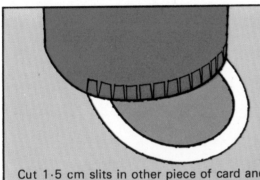

Cut 1·5 cm slits in other piece of card and bend tabs upwards. Glue tabs inside rim of hat to make peak. Paint the hat.

6

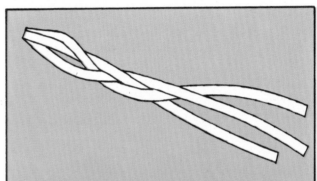

Glue three strips of paper together at one end and plait them *loosely*. Glue other ends together.

7

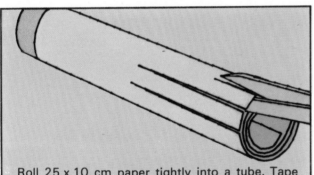

Roll 25 x 10 cm paper tightly into a tube. Tape one end firmly. Cut 7·5 cm deep slits, 0·5 cm apart in outside layer of paper.

8

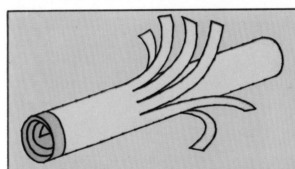

Curl strips out. Cut more slits and curl out. Continue cutting and curling. Pull middle of tube occasionally to make longer.

9

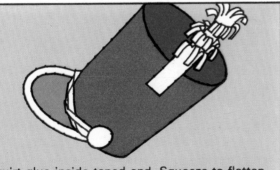

Squirt glue inside taped end. Squeeze to flatten. Glue to side of hat. Glue on plait. Cut 2 2·5-cm discs. Glue on ends of plait.

10

Cut 1 cm slits around edge of paper circles, 0·5 cm apart. Bend alternate tabs slightly. Glue large one to front hat and small one to plume.

11

Crusader Castle

YOU WILL NEED:
large cardboard grocery box
small cardboard box
cardboard box: approx. 25 x 10 x 10 cm
4 round washing-up liquid bottles
2 drinking straws
paper · paints · scissors · pencil
craft knife · steel rule · glue
2 toilet roll tubes
card: approx. 18 x 5 cm
fine string 30 cm long

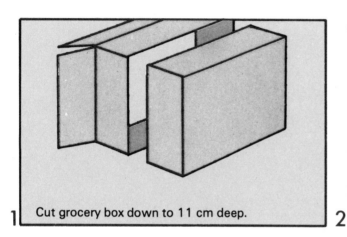

1 Cut grocery box down to 11 cm deep.

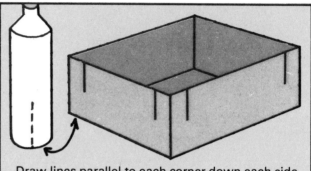

2 Draw lines parallel to each corner down each side of box, the same width as half the bottle. Cut half way down these lines.

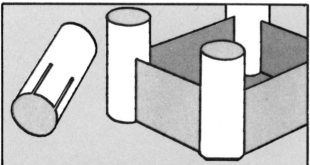

3 Cut the top and bottom from each bottle. Cut 2 slots 5 cm deep, 6·5 cm apart at one end of each bottle. Slide bottles on to corners.

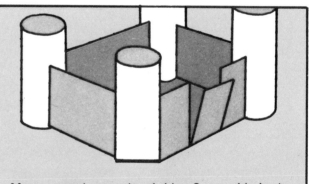

4 Measure and cut a drawbridge 9 cm wide in the middle of one side.

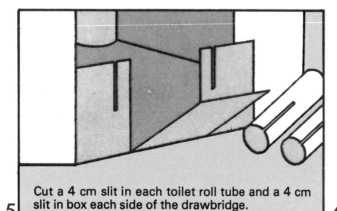

5 Cut a 4 cm slit in each toilet roll tube and a 4 cm slit in box each side of the drawbridge.

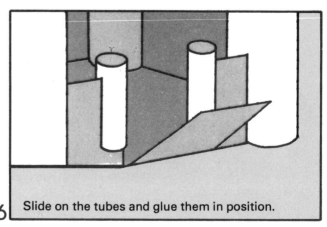

6 Slide on the tubes and glue them in position.

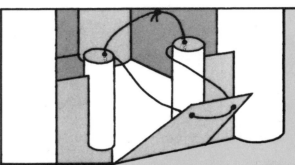

7 Make 2 holes in top of drawbridge and 1 hole in each toilet roll tube near the top at the back.

8 Thread each end of string through holes in drawbridge, through holes in tubes and out of the top. Tie ends together.

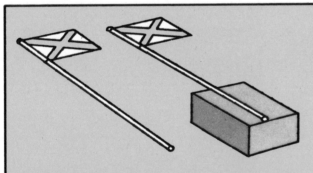

9 Cut 2 slits 1·5 cm deep, in the top of each tube and insert the piece of card. Make sure knotted string is behind it.

10 Cut top off long box and cut a door as shown. Glue to middle of fort.

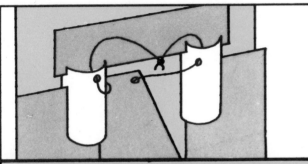

11 Paint and cut out flags 6 x 4 cm from paper. Glue to ends of straws. Glue one to small box.

12 Cut battlements on all walls and turrets. Glue small box and flag inside tower and other flag in drawbridge tower. Paint castle.

A Country Farm...

YOU WILL NEED:
wood or hardboard: approx. 120 x 60 cm
cardboard box: approx. 18 x 23 x 5 cm
cardboard box: approx. 9 x 12 x 4 cm
cardboard box: 20 x 20 x 28 cm · cardboard
   box: 25 x 5 x 2·5 cm
thick card: 33 x 33 cm · hay or dried grass
piece of old sheet: approx. 30 x 38 cm
newspaper · piece of nylon foam: approx. 45 x 45 x 4 cm
strong glue · drinking straws · corrugated card
paints · scissors · craft knife · kitchen foil · card
pencil · Emulsion paint · ruler

1 Glue larger box at a corner of board. Glue 9 x 12 x 4 cm box in the middle of it. Roll up newspaper and glue it round the bottom box.

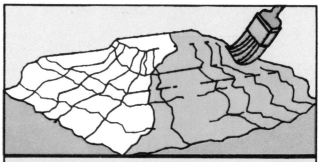

2 Cover boxes with material and glue into place. Don't attempt to make material smooth — it should be ruffled. Coat with Emulsion.

3 Cut 2 pieces of corrugated card — shape as above and glue to board. Paint them brown. Paint footpath and then rest of board green.

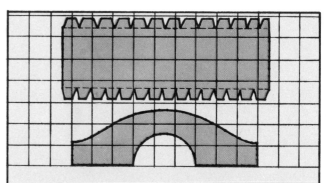

4 Cut the above pieces from card and fold as shown.

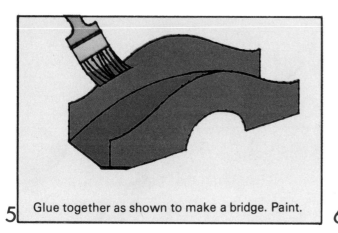

5 Glue together as shown to make a bridge. Paint.

6 Tear a piece of kitchen foil, and glue it to board, to make a stream. Glue bridge over it.

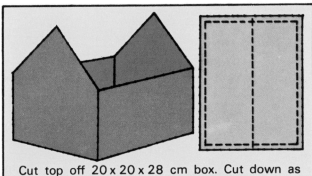

Cut top off 20 x 20 x 28 cm box. Cut down as shown. Measure X and Y. Draw 2 rectangles on card to these measurements. Add 1 cm all round.

7

Fold card in middle. Glue to house as roof. Cut hole in side and glue along box in place. Paint house. Glue on hay for thatch.

8

Cut trees and hedges from nylon foam and paint. Make fences from pieces of drinking straw glued together.

9

Glue fences, farmhouse and trees to board. Turn over page and make farm animals to go in your farm.

10

...and Farm Animals

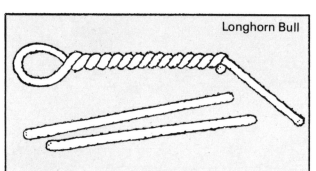

Longhorn Bull

1 Bend a 2 cm loop about 10 cm along a pipe cleaner. Wind ends together and bend end as shown. Cut other pipe cleaner in half.

2 Twist each half into first one to make legs. Wrap cotton wool round body between legs (more underneath than on top).

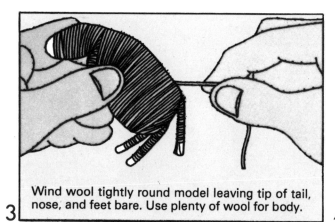

3 Wind wool tightly round model leaving tip of tail, nose, and feet bare. Use plenty of wool for body.

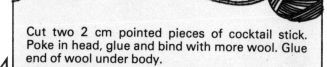

4 Cut two 2 cm pointed pieces of cocktail stick. Poke in head, glue and bind with more wool. Glue end of wool under body.

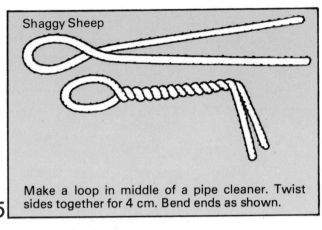

Shaggy Sheep

5 Make a loop in middle of a pipe cleaner. Twist sides together for 4 cm. Bend ends as shown.

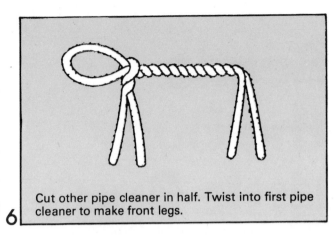

6 Cut other pipe cleaner in half. Twist into first pipe cleaner to make front legs.

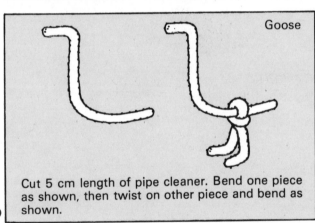

7 Wind black wool round head and neck, leaving nose bare. Glue end under neck.

8 Spread glue along back. Fold 5 cm piece of cotton wool over back and 'comb' it lightly with sandpaper to fluff it out.

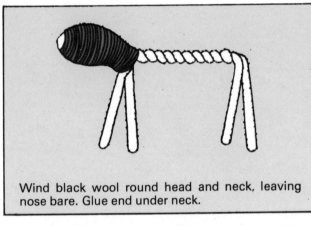

Goose

9 Cut 5 cm length of pipe cleaner. Bend one piece as shown, then twist on other piece and bend as shown.

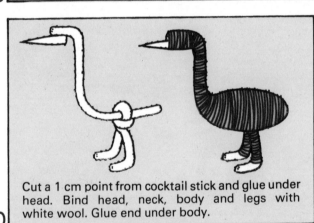

10 Cut a 1 cm point from cocktail stick and glue under head. Bind head, neck, body and legs with white wool. Glue end under body.

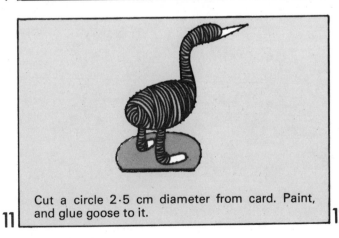

11 Cut a circle 2·5 cm diameter from card. Paint, and glue goose to it.

12 Poke holes in sides of body with cocktail stick and glue feathers in place.

Bertie the Busy Little Bug

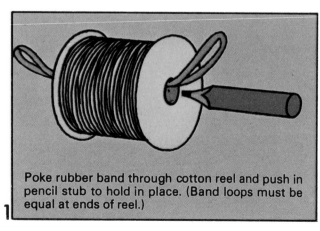

1 Poke rubber band through cotton reel and push in pencil stub to hold in place. (Band loops must be equal at ends of reel.)

2 Glue pencil in place. Pierce a small hole on each side of the dish near the rim.

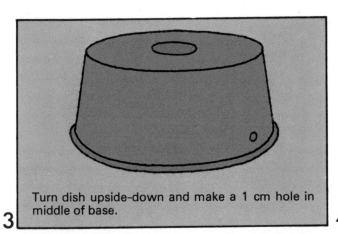

3 Turn dish upside-down and make a 1 cm hole in middle of base.

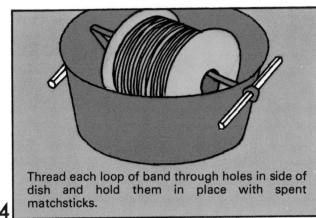

4 Thread each loop of band through holes in side of dish and hold them in place with spent matchsticks.

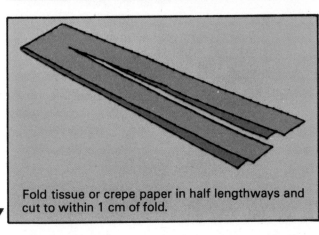

5 Thread end of cotton through hole in base and tie it to 8 cm dowel or pencil.

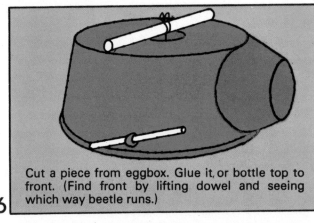

6 Cut a piece from eggbox. Glue it, or bottle top to front. (Find front by lifting dowel and seeing which way beetle runs.)

7 Fold tissue or crepe paper in half lengthways and cut to within 1 cm of fold.

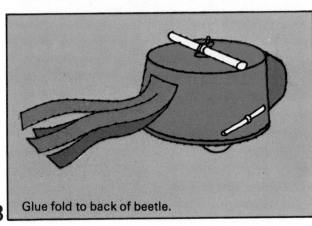

8 Glue fold to back of beetle.

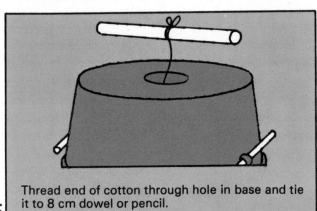

9 Paint the beetle.

10 To make beetle scurry along, lift dowel and lower it slowly. Beetle runs best on carpet.

41

4-6-8 Special Express

YOU WILL NEED:
wood or Balsa wood: approx. 72 x 5 x 1 cm
cardboard box: approx. 10 x 7 x 15 cm
cardboard box: approx. 10 x 7 x 20 cm
round plastic bottle: approx. 25 x 6·5 diameter
stiff card: approx. 33 x 10 cm
6 jar lids: approx. 6 cm diameter · sandpaper
4 drinking straws · egg box · 4 1-cm nails
pins · cardboard tube · strong glue · saw · compass · ruler
craft knife · oil paints · brushes · hammer · scissors
2 small bottle caps · countersink bit or file
2 matchboxes · threaded hook and eye

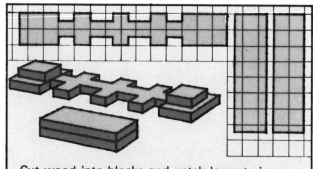

1 Cut wood into blocks and notch largest piece as shown. Glue matchboxes 0·5 cm from each end. Glue 2 smaller pieces together.

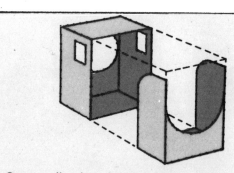

2 Cut smaller box in half (through 15 cm side). Shape 1 half as shown. Cut small windows in 'cab'. Cut holes same diameter as bottle.

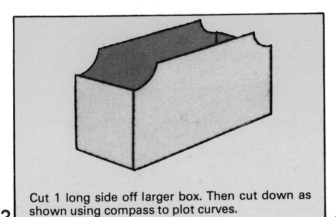

3 Cut 1 long side off larger box. Then cut down as shown using compass to plot curves.

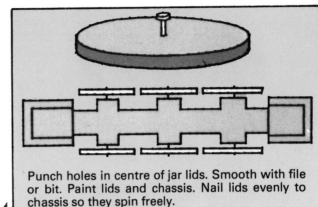

4 Punch holes in centre of jar lids. Smooth with file or bit. Paint lids and chassis. Nail lids evenly to chassis so they spin freely.

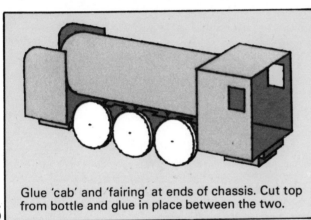

5 Glue 'cab' and 'fairing' at ends of chassis. Cut top from bottle and glue in place between the two.

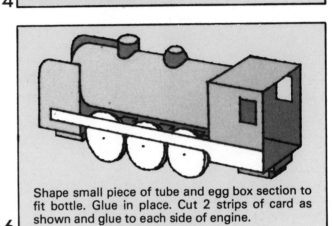

6 Shape small piece of tube and egg box section to fit bottle. Glue in place. Cut 2 strips of card as shown and glue to each side of engine.

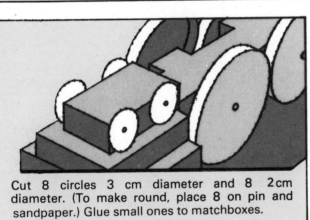

7 Cut 8 circles 3 cm diameter and 8 2cm diameter. (To make round, place 8 on pin and sandpaper.) Glue small ones to matchboxes.

8 Paint remaining block of wood. Nail larger circles to it, measuring position carefully. Glue to tender. Paint tender.

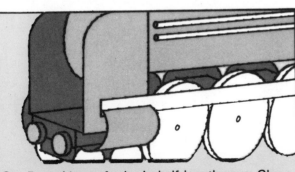

9 Cut 5 cm piece of tube in half lengthways. Glue to each side of engine at front. Glue on straw 'pipes' and bottle cap 'buffers'.

10 Finish painting model. Screw hook to engine chassis and eye to tender. Make carriages and trucks in same way as tender.

Heavy Duty Crane

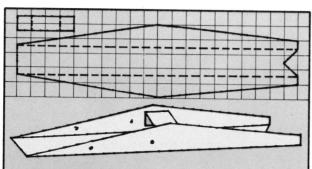

1 Glue down flaps of one box, and cut off one large side. Cut 4 strips, 6 cm wide from this and fold as shown.

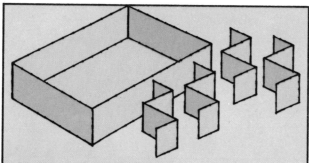

2 Glue pieces inside corners of box. Make hole 1 cm from top. Push pencil stubs through outer hole, cotton reel and inner hole. Glue to card.

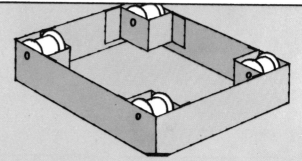

3 Cut above shapes from card. Score and bend along dotted lines. Glue small piece inside long one. Pierce 4 small holes as shown.

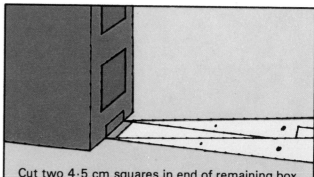

4 Cut two 4·5 cm squares in end of remaining box. Open out flaps at other end. Sellotape jib to corner of cab on top and underneath.

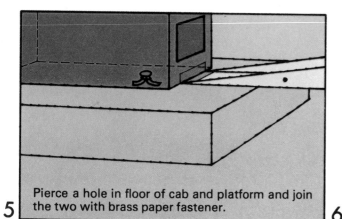

5 Pierce a hole in floor of cab and platform and join the two with brass paper fastener.

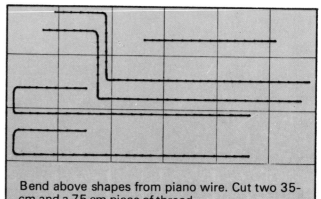

6 Bend above shapes from piano wire. Cut two 35-cm and a 75 cm piece of thread.

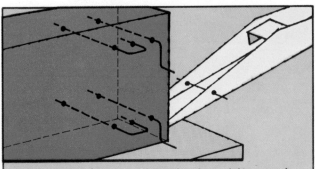

Make holes in each side of cab and insert wire pieces. Push short piece through lower holes in jib and glue it.

7

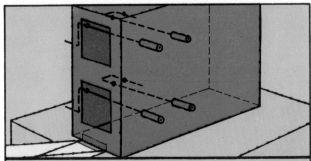

Wind Sellotape round ends of wire. Handles should not slide sideways. Other two pieces should slide 1 cm from side to side.

8

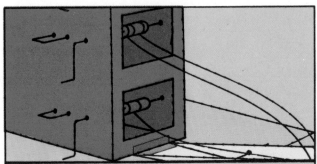

Wind Sellotape round middle of each handle to make fatter. Glue 2 short threads to top handle and long thread to bottom handle.

9

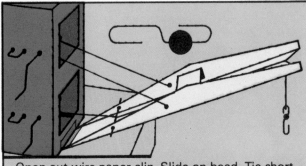

Open out wire paper clip. Slide on bead. Tie short threads to jib. Poke long thread under jib wire and cross strut. Tie on hook. Weight back. Glue flaps.

10